Pre-
2u

To: Ms. Kim

With Love: Your Class!

Thank You Teacher

by
Marianne Richmond

To Ms Kim

From Pre-K class

Date 2007-2008

Every year before school starts, we kids wonder who our teacher will be...

'cause that decision pretty much shapes the year.

I'm
really
glad I got
you for
my teacher.

Thanks for everything you do to make our classroom really great.

Thank you for recognizing
my unique talents and abilities...

and for

encouraging

me in those areas.

Thank you, too, for helping me when
I have a hard time with stuff.

Thanks for mixing up
the learning time with
good humor and silliness.

And for making things fun and
interesting when you could.

(I know some subjects just aren't
that fascinating.)

Thank you
for your
patience.

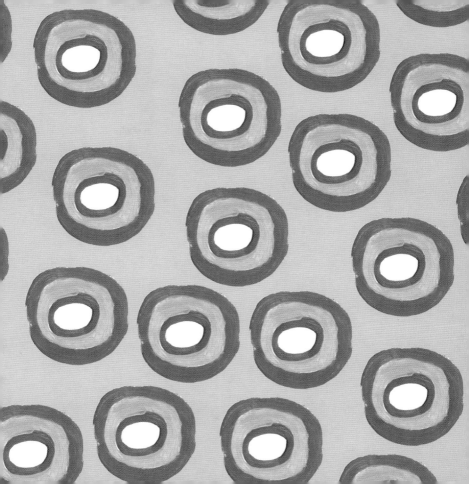

Thanks for showing up
day after day –
especially on a day when
you know things might be

challenging or stressful.

your students...
and for
talking me up
to my family.

Thanks for helping me feel proud of me, too.

Thank you
for all your
behind-the-scenes
work.

Learning new
things.
Grading papers.
Planning.

Thank you *for* letting

us **benefit** from all

the classes

you have taught

before us.

But not
comparing
us.

Thank you for
showing me possibilities,
encouraging creativity
and accepting mistakes.

Thanks for liking what you do.

It shows.

It's especially great when you

get excited 'cause one of us

did
something
that

shows
we
paid

attention.

Teachers have no idea how far their influence goes.

Just so you know,
I've learned
so much from you
that I will
take with me.

Thank You Teacher

Marianne Richmond Studios, Inc.
3900 Stinson Boulevard NE
Minneapolis, MN 55421
www.mariannerichmond.com

ISBN 10: 0-9763101-0-4
ISBN 13: 978-0-9763101-0-5

Illustrations by Marianne Richmond

Book design by Sara Dare Biscan

Printed in China

Third Printing

Also available from author & illustrator
Marianne Richmond:

The Gift of an Angel
The Gift of a Memory
Hooray for You!
The Gifts of Being Grand
I Love You So...
Dear Daughter
Dear Son
Dear Granddaughter
Dear Grandson
My Shoes Take Me Where I Want to Go
Fish Kisses and Gorilla Hugs
I Love You so Much...
Happy Birthday to You!
I Wished for You, an adoption story
You are my Wish come True

To learn more about Marianne's products,
please visit
www.mariannerichmond.com